HOW TO RAISE GREAT KIDS

101 Fun & Easy Ideas

JIM GROMER

How to Raise Great Kids

Jim Gromer
Author/Screenwriter
Facebook: How to Raise Great Kids
Email: GreatKids101@gmail.com

www.GreatKids101.com

ISBN-13: 978-0-9964907-8-8

Editors: Barb Gromer & Rachel Gromer

Cover: Agata Porebska, www.Bukovero.com
Interior: Lisa Cerasoli & Danielle Canfield

United States of America
Printed and bound in the United States of America

Books are available in quantity for promotional use.

First Edition

"It is not what you do for your children, but what you have taught them to do for themselves that will make them successful human beings."

—Ann Landers

This book is dedicated
to all of the wonderful parents trying
to make the world a better place
by raising disciplined, hard-working,
and respectful kids.

I want to thank my parents for being
excellent teachers, my wife for
being amazing, and my own children
for being great test subjects.

Introduction

One cool August evening, my beautiful wife and I shared with our kids some of what we hoped to teach them in life. I said, "a solid work ethic," and Rachel told them, "a deep faith."

Then my son chimed in, "I want to leave my daughter my warm smelly socks!"

Life is messy but when you cherish the golden moments and power through the inevitable tough times, you give your family a fighting chance to leave a positive legacy. Kids develop the majority of their personalities by age 7, so it is never too early to start or too late to try. Before you know it, your kids will be all grown up and moved out (hopefully). Do your very best to make the most of it!

Since we think your family is so amazing, we put together our favorite 101 fun and easy ideas to help you and your kids to be happier, more productive, and better prepared for life's challenges. These won't work for all age groups but the principles remain the same. Hopefully, these ideas will only spur you on to bigger and better daily teachable moments for your potential packed squirts. Your influence shrinks with each passing year so take advantage of every opportunity to love, instruct, and encourage your children while they still trust you to lead the way.

We regularly go out of our way to NOT make life fair for our kids, because life isn't fair in the least. However, for many of these games, it is best to let different children win each game as regularly as possible. If one youngster loses even a few times at any particular challenge, he or she probably won't want to play it again ever. Your kids are smarter than you think!

The investments you make now in your child's life will have costly consequences or pay off enormously. The simple fact that you picked up this type of book tells me that you're highly intelligent and most likely extremely attractive. Congratulations on your commitment to parenting well.

We know you can do it!

How to Raise Great Kids
101 Fun & Easy Ideas

1

Freebie

Starting today and every day moving forward, allow your kids to tell you anything at any time without getting in any trouble. Before your head pops off, please let me explain.

We call them "Freebies" and it has been one of the best things we've done for our family. My wife and I promise not to tell anyone or to punish our children for coming clean about anything.

This does several amazing things. First, it builds trust so your daughter will come to you with her problems without worrying about getting busted. Second, she becomes comfortable talking with you about uncomfortable topics. If her friends or authority figures are dabbling with inappropriate drugs, sex, or alcohol, don't you want her to come to you first about it?

Then you decide with her the best course of action moving forward. Should you tell someone's parents? Report it to authorities? Help her find new friends? Or should your daughter be punished for what she's done? The bottom line is that you get to help her make good choices and work through potentially destructive problems together.

This should be one of your top priorities as a great parent!

2

Yes, Sir/ Ma'am

One of the greatest rules we came up with was teaching our kids to always say, "Yes, ma'am" and "Yes, sir" when we ask them to do anything. They must politely agree first before they can offer up another option.

If we ask our son to clean his room, he needs to reply, "Yes, sir," before he may ask, "Can I please clean my room after I finish my game?" We teach him the importance of being obedient, but we also give him the freedom to have a say in the matter.

Of course, you could drop the "sir" and the "ma'am," but we can't stress the importance of this particular suggestion enough. Who wants a disrespectful child who tells you "No" whenever you ask for something?

You don't want to raise frightened little robots, but obedience should be a top priority in your household.

3

Your Job as Parent

One of your main jobs is to prepare your child for the responsibility and independence of being a grown-up. This includes teaching him self-control, healthy habits, and hard work. Yes, hard work!

If you teach your toddler that TV, video games, and play-time are job #1, he'll make that his top priority today, in high school, and beyond as well. Trust us, you don't want that! So please try to make his chores fun, teach him to do his own laundry (our nine-year-old does his), and, hopefully, you'll raise a happy, healthy, and productive family.

We started by having our three-year-old stand on a step-stool and put away the silverware from the dishwasher (after we cleaned out the sharp stuff). Now he does it without a fuss! With a little patience and a whole lot of consistency, you'll soon have hard-working kids who don't flip out when asked to help.

Just look at any farming family for the possibilities in your own home.

4

Parent First and Friend Second

Your child desperately needs you to be a parent first and a friend second.

If you need your little one's approval to feel good about yourself, you daily risk spoiling her. The best parents recognize consistent discipline is essential for raising great kids. Now would be a good time to get on the same page as your significant other as well. If your daughter learns to go to daddy when mommy says "No," the effectiveness of both parents suffers.

Your child doesn't need a best buddy, she needs someone who will prepare her for the challenges of adulthood. That includes a solid work ethic, independence, and an awareness of the world that will help her become successful, happy, and wise. This book was designed to assist in that process. Feel free to improve on these ideas and take them to the next level in an effort to raise wonderful human beings. It's not going to be easy, but it will be rewarding for both of you.

So correct your little one when she misbehaves and discipline her with love. Play with her, be silly with her, and enjoy her friendship often but please be a parent first.

5

Leaving a Proper Message

We regularly play games at dinner and the winner gets out of doing dishes. I wish I could win more often!

This game teaches your son how to leave an appropriate voicemail message. Have him recite a proper greeting, the important information, and a decent sign-off. If you don't teach him, who will?

Give different reasons for leaving a message and award players a letter grade. If he needs to leave a phone number, tell him to give it twice and to speak slowly. We typically give a lot of A's and B's with some A++'s but no D's or F's. Remember again to spread the wins around if you have multiple kids. It's okay to explain to older siblings in private that you are splitting up the victories to keep the younger ones engaged.

Don't let them tell the toddlers about this though. That's just not nice!

6

Three Questions

Did you ever wonder why kids' toothpaste-makers chose electric blue with sparkles for the color? It sure doesn't match any of our sinks and it's a nightmare to scrape off. Sorry, I get sidetracked sometimes with my deep thoughts.

We came up with another fun idea that helps our kids interact with adults. We call it "Three Questions," and we regularly ask our children to participate with anyone and everyone.

"Where do you work?" is a good icebreaker, but our kids must ask a typical question about life, the weather, sports, or any other generally accepted topic. Then they need to ask two intelligent follow-up questions. You'll be amazed and impressed as your little one learns to talk appropriately with grown-ups.

The cell phones come soon enough so please teach your little one how to communicate effectively today using this or a similar game while you still have influence. We encourage intelligent texting from our oldest and she understands we crack down on bad grammar, misspellings, and poor punctuation as well.

Some of her friends' texts can't even be decoded because the spelling is so bad!

7

Boys and Bathrooms

If you only have daughters, you can thankfully skip this recommendation but for those of you with boys, please start this one today.

Every time your son misses the mark or forgets to put up the seat before he whizzes, immediately have him clean the toilet and the floor around it. We have our boys use a wet wipe but a paper towel with Lysol works, too. Instruct him how to aim for the water or take responsibility for missing the mark. It's never too early to include him in helping scrub the toilet anyway even if he does aim like Robin Hood.

If you cook, clean, and buy everything for him, why wouldn't he want to live with you into his thirties!?!

Heck, I would, too!

8

Eat in the Kitchen

My wife and I only allow our kids to eat in the kitchen or outdoors.

Yes, you can do whatever you want as with all of these humble suggestions, but when the spaghetti ends up on your new carpet, you'll be reminded of this advice. When you move the couch and find a slice of pizza—you get the idea. This is a tough rule to keep and you can certainly make exceptions, but life is so much easier when you don't have to worry about possible food messes in every room.

If you do make an exception to this or any rule, your little mess-makers will inevitably look for loopholes in all of your brilliant suggestions.

9

Give Them the Power

When someone makes fun of our kids or upsets them, we call that "giving them the power." In a perfect world, kids would be nice and no one would say mean things to your beautiful, smart, and wonderful child, but that's simply not reality. Teach your youngsters early and often to not let other people bother them with their insults and jealousy.

If serious bullying exists, you need to talk to a teacher, the bully, and the parents when appropriate. No child should suffer this kind of mistreatment, but recognize that most harassment comes from hurting kids who try to hurt other kids. Encourage your daughter not to let these words bother her whenever possible.

Don't give others the power to upset your kid, and that goes for grown-ups, too!

10

Cleaning Schedule

This isn't so much about making your child's life easier as it is making *your* life easier. Your little one gets the benefit of hard work and a tidy house, and you get the simplicity of a manageable schedule.

Try to deep clean one area of your house every two weeks. Put a specific room on your calendar or in your smart phone, and stick to the plan. This end-of-the-month, we are cleaning under the coach, wiping down baseboards, and dusting the bookshelves in our living room. Hiring a maid isn't an option for most of us and following this twice-a-month schedule makes house cleaning that much easier.

And make your child help out, too!

11

Top Five

We love this one! My wife and I play this game together almost as much (if not more) as we play it with our family.

Each person answers the same question in "Top Five" as you each come up with your favorite foods, books, places to visit, smells, places you've been, or favorite things about someone. Take turns picking new subjects as you share your fabulous fives about everything under the sun.

The topics can be endless as you and your youngster enjoy learning more about the things your family loves most.

12

Claim a Geographical Location

We claimed Gromer Creek!

It's really called Cherry Creek but we slapped our last name on it, and my kids absolutely love going down there to splash, play, and get messy.

Your spot could be a playground, a pond, or a slice of the ocean but make it yours, and allow your son to explore and play to his heart's content. We've seen snakes and crawdads, hiked upstream in our bare feet, and built castles in the sand. It's priceless!

Now every time we pass by, my kids rave about how much they love Gromer Creek.

13

Family Trivia

Celebrate some of your favorite memories with this clever contest.

Each person shares an event and the others try to guess who was involved. For example, ask which member of your family used to wear an *Incredibles* costume and wanted to be called "Dash" for a whole year. These can be silly but try to focus on the accomplishments and the high points more than the embarrassing stuff. Nobody likes to be made fun of.

If you're going to pick on anyone, confess your silly stuff and not theirs. And if you have an only child, ask her to guess her grandparents', relatives', or your accomplishments. Whoever guesses correctly gets to go next.

This also provides a good opportunity to talk about reputation and how other people see you and your little one outside the family. It takes a lifetime to build up a good reputation but just one stupid act to tear it all down.

14

Start a Book

This is one of our kids' favorites!

Before they were born (but it's never too late to start), we began writing in a journal for them. We record their accomplishments, funny things they say, as well as the greatest moments of their lives. Each child gets his own book.

Now we spend whole dinnertimes reading the amazing things they've done. Use it to encourage them, to record milestones, and to look back at the highlights of your time together.

My parents put some stories in my baby book when I was little, and I cherish them to this day.

15

Build a Fort

Teach your little architect about structural integrity and creativity by making a fort.

Grab blankets, pillows, and flashlights for an entertaining afternoon. Bonus points are awarded for getting down on all fours and crawling around in there, but enter at your own risk!

Seriously, please use caution when stacking things to hold blankets in place. Books, toys, and weights can all come crashing down when the roof gets tugged. How long the fort stays up may also be a problem, so lay down some ground rules before construction begins to avoid unnecessary tears.

Happy building!

16

Initials

This popular car game involves asking "yes" or "no" questions to find the correct answer.

Start by giving only the initials of the name you want them to guess. W.S. would be William Shakespeare, and B.L. would be Buzz Lightyear. Sample questions include, "Is it a real person?" and "Is it a woman?" Or they could ask, "Do we know him personally?"

You can use proper names, foods, or any topic you choose, and you'll joyfully be at your destination before you know it!

17

How to Pick a TV Show or Movie

When your son has a friend over or if you have more than one child, this is the best way to pick an age-appropriate show or movie.

First, have kids pick out three movies. Next, each one gets to choose one movie that he didn't originally pick. He can only select from the others' choices. Take the chosen movies and everyone gets to pick out one favorite even if it was his original choice. Obviously, this works better with an odd number of participants but the decision becomes easier once the field has been narrowed.

Mom or dad gets the final say if there isn't a clear winner, but at least it will be a program most of them said "yes" to at least once.

18

Curses! Car Game

Curses! is based on the popular Worldwise Imports board game, but our family found a fun way to play it on the road.

Please consider buying the real game but to play in the car, simply come up with a silly "curse" and assign it to one person. The curse should be simple, kind, and funny. One example would be, "Scratch your armpits like an ape whenever you speak." If someone doesn't obey her curse three times, she is out.

Careful what you plague other people with because it could just come back to haunt you!

19

How to Read

The Conviction to Lead by Albert Mohler says, "You should read a book or article *only* for what it's worth"[1] (emphasis added).

Please don't just teach your kids how to read, show them why they should read. With so much information, little readers need to know how to make the best use of their time by understanding the what, why, and how of reading.

First, help him understand *what* he is reading. Is it for fun? Is it for school or for more information on how to do something?

Second, help him understand *why* the authors wrote what they did. What information should he learn? What's the point?

Third, teach him *how* he should read. Instruct your little booklover to treat reading just like he would eating healthy.

---

[1] Albert Mohler, *The Conviction to Lead* (Bloomington, MN: Bethany House Publishing, 2012), 101.

It's okay to have some desserts but he also needs meats and veggies, too.

Lastly, your little scholar doesn't have to read *every* word of every book he picks up. He can do that, but he should learn to be a smart shopper when it comes to reading. Show him how to read critically, to find the main points, and to recognize what can be skimmed over. If he wants to read every word and he has the time, then by all means, let him.

20

How to Handle a Bully

Along with teaching your child to stand up for herself, it is important to show her how to stand up to a bully. Every school has them, most neighborhoods, and some workplaces do, too. Mean people stink and they can make life miserable!

ATA Martial Arts in Colorado taught our little ones something I'll never forget. If another kid is being bullied, have your child simply walk up, put an arm around the victim, and walk away together. It solves most situations and your little superhero doesn't even need to battle the offending super villain.

Also, work with your child on how she should handle someone who makes fun of her. Practice at home and make sure she knows when to walk away, when to get the help of a parent or teacher, and when to stand up for herself.

You simply can't avoid this type of schmuck so you might as well learn how to deal with them early. Sadly!

21

What I Like About You!

Pick one person in the family and have everyone, including that person, say his favorite thing about her.

This offers great insight and encouragement for everyone. Your child learns what characteristics are most important to you, and you get a glimpse of what means the most to her. If the selected person can't come up with something positive about herself, then deeper issues may exist.

Everyone should have at least a basic level of self-confidence, otherwise steps to fix the misperception should be taken immediately.

22

Sports Perspective

I hate to break it to you, but your son probably won't be among the .0001% of the population who gets to play professional sports for a living. Sorry!

Of course, you should discuss with your significant other whether to get your youngster into sports, theater, or music, but check your motives at the door. If you try to live vicariously through him and think Tiger Woods' dad was smart for pushing Tiger so hard, remember how it turned out for Tiger. He was a professional success and a personal failure.

All I'm saying is to encourage your son to do everything he attempts well, but please don't let anything get out of balance. Give him every opportunity to be successful but hug him hard when he falls short. The most important lessons in youth sports should always be teamwork, player and character development, and a healthy lifestyle.

If he actually goes pro, congrats!

23

Just One Bite

Fighting the food battle can be frustrating but please have your child taste one bite of everything. If our finicky eater won't at least try it, we change it to two or three bites instead.

If you must banish your daughter to the naughty corner for at least not trying what's on the menu, tell her she still has to take a bite when she comes back from serving time. You'll be surprised at how quickly your little one catches on to what's expected of her.

On a disgusting side note, we let our son spit the bite into a napkin if he truly hates it. He would literally gag on certain foods and nobody should have to endure that.

Poor little dude, but he tasted everything we asked him to.

24

Shark Tank

Play a game based on the popular TV show *Shark Tank*, and challenge your children to come up with a new business or invention.

Encourage them to create a new and interesting concept, and try to sell it in a convincing manner. We ask our kids for an introduction, a specific dollar amount in return for part of their company, and a pitch. It's always a good idea to explore these types of concepts with your offspring, and the idea isn't nearly as important as the presentation. All of us need to be salesmen in one sense or another, so why not start when they're young?

Their little plans may actually lead to some big bucks for both of you!

25

Water Drinking Contest

Sometimes your son will get cranky simply because he is dehydrated. When one of our little angels acts like the devil, we usually start with water.

We'll even have a water-drinking contest to see who can drink the longest. Please stop him from floating away if he doesn't stop on his own, but you get the idea. A couple ounces of water or juice go a long way toward maintaining happier healthier children.

It's also okay for you to ask if his pee is dark yellow or to look before he flushes. That's usually a pretty good indicator if he isn't getting enough liquids.

Clear pee means he's probably good to go—literally!

26

What Not to Wear

Parents battle needlessly about what their little fashion statements wear. Why!?!

You bought, borrowed, or stole all of her clothes anyway, why not let her express herself? If you really hate something she puts on, just have it magically disappear the next time you do laundry. Ta-da! Problem solved.

If you let her choose most days, then you get the right to tell her what to wear on other occasions. "I let you wear whatever you wanted last week, so mommy gets to pick what you wear today."

And she needs to agree. After all, you're still the boss (or you should be). You certainly shouldn't be battling every day over what not to wear. If it's freezing outside, don't ask her if she wants a jacket, just put one on her.

If you ask, she just might say, "No, thank you!"

Then what!?!

27

Date Night

If you spend all day, every day pouring into your children, you'll probably burn out. No matter how fun, well behaved, and brilliant your offspring may be, you should regularly be making time for yourself and your significant other as well. For the single parents, you deserve a break today, too!

Yes, babysitters are expensive but it's cheaper than divorce. Make time this week for your spouse even if it means putting the little one in his room early and just making brownies together. Your child needs love and attention, but so does your soul mate. Massages, long walks, and dessert together are all little things that make a big difference.

And if being a stay-home mother or father isn't for you, please go back to work even if it's only part-time. Your sanity might just be worth the massive cost of daycare. Maybe you work, but you'd rather stay home with the kids. If you can pull it off financially, why not try it? Your opinion counts even if your better half disagrees.

Figure out what is best for *everyone* and go for it!

28

How Can I Be a Better Parent?

Want to know the easiest technique for knocking this child rearing thing out of the park? Ask your little professor.

As long as you don't bite her head off when she tells you, you should get some fairly honest answers from a real expert. I simply ask, "What can I do to be a better daddy?" The answers reveal so much about how I'm doing this week. I've learned that I need to have more patience, play more games with her, and schedule a Daddy Date with her immediately. I can do that.

You'll be pleasantly surprised to hear how you can improve today.

29

Play Dates

I grew up in the days when kids joyfully disappeared after school and came home when it got dark. It was great, but we live in different times now.

Some parents have become so overprotective that children have no choice but to stay inside, play video games, or plop down in front of the flat screen. Please push your son outside as much as possible to play and explore. Also, actively seek play dates with other kids his age. He needs to learn to get along, work together, and simply find ways to entertain himself.

A good friend of mine recently admitted that his company has trouble finding employees who can carry on a conversation, talk and write professionally, and simply interact with clients. You need to go out of your way to help your children socialize, problem solve, and make new friends.

Both of your futures might just depend on it!

30

Staycation

Most of you have already heard about this one, but try taking it to a whole new level.

Pretend you live in another state and are interested in visiting your own hometown. Aside from picking the hotel, what would you like to do? What would you want to see? Where would you take your little ones?

Jump on the Internet, pick up a travel book, or ask friends about the best attractions in your neck of the woods. Sometimes the best adventures are right in your own back-yard!

31

Learn to Ride a Bike

Learning to ride a bike can be very intimidating for your daughter. She has to steer, peddle, and try to figure out how to stop all while balancing on two skinny wheels.

Our experience taught us that training wheels are the most difficult way to figure it out, but it's better than nothing. Hands down, the easiest way to teach your daughter to ride is to buy a balance bike without pedals. ABC's *Shark Tank* featured these bikes with the KaZam brand but several companies make them now. If it fits into your budget, your child can learn to steer and glide without having to worry about pedaling, too. It's brilliant!

The best *place* to learn to ride a bike is at a local high school track. As long as the track team isn't using it, your kid can safely scoot around without worrying about cars, sidewalks, and those pesky mailboxes.

The only problem is that our six-year-old only knows how to make right turns!

32

Riddles/Jokes

It's very important for your son to learn to talk to adults. He needs to interact with teachers, friends' parents, and even strangers such as restaurant or grocery store workers. If he is so shy that he can't effectively communicate, it could cause problems down the road.

We taught our children at a young age to tell one simple joke to help them get over this nervousness. They learned to be more comfortable interacting with grown-ups, and the adults got a good chuckle out of it. Here is one of our favorites.

"Knock-knock."
"Who's there?"
"Olive."
"Olive who?"
"Olive you!"

Or maybe your youngster prefers a riddle. "What's red and smells like blue paint?" The answer is red paint. You get the idea, and you could certainly go online to find something that suits your personal sense of humor.

It's cute, easy, and now we regularly get compliments about our children's ability to chat with anyone.

33

Directions Home

It's never too early to start teaching your daughter about her surroundings and how to get home. We regularly share what streets we are on, what landmarks are around, and the different ways we can use to find our way back.

Do you really want your sixteen-year-old relying on her smart phone to get everywhere? Or would you rather she knew the lay of the land fairly well by the time she earns her almighty driver's permit?

Your little navigator should be familiar enough to help her friends' parents find your home as well. It's never too soon to start learning and we regularly ask our kids how to get us back.

34

Red Car Alert

Help your son learn his colors by playing this clever car game.

Pick a common color, watch for a truck or car of that variety, and keep your eyes peeled. We say we are on a "Red Car Alert!" Whoever sees one first gets to pick next. You could choose a color *and* the type of vehicle to make it more difficult. For example, pick a yellow motorcycle or a blue truck.

We did have to make a rule to prevent players who suggest a color from magically seeing one right after they've picked it. That's no fun!

35

Road Signs

Here is another great game for preparing safe teenage drivers (safer, I should say).

Start by picking a particular sign to watch for—*Speed Limit, Stop Sign, Yield,* etc. Your child learns what they mean and why. The first person who discovers one gets to pick the next sign. You may have to help choose the sign though, because some signs don't appear very often.

Don't be surprised if you get a little help going the speed limit the next time you drive as well!

36

Attitude is Everything

We regularly ask our kids, "What's the most important thing?" The correct answer is "Attitude."

If he is tackling a challenge, facing a tough circumstance, or struggling with a relationship, we gently remind him that he can often control how it affects him. As I say this, my ten-year-old is trying to pull my six-year-old's loose tooth. Another perfect example of when "Attitude is everything."

Life is tough, but it's a whole lot more manageable when you have a positive attitude. Explain this to your child and expect the best, but be okay when you get the worst.

Everybody has an off-day and we all need a little extra space when we do.

37

Keeping Activities in Check

Does your little dynamo go straight from school to Taekwondo, to swim team, a quick bite of dinner, then it's right off to ukulele lessons? You may be stressing your poor kid out.

If it's straining for you to just taxi her around, what do you think it's doing to her!?! My wife and I do our best to limit our busybodies to one or two extracurricular activities at a time. Once you add homework, friends, and family events, kids can get just as overwhelmed as we are.

However, our children normally handle it a little better than we do!

38

Healthy Hands

Want a healthier household? Please teach your son how to wash his hands properly and have him scrub often.

Too much hand sanitizer may be bad for you, but we'll let you decide how to handle that. We just respectfully encourage you to have your child wash his hands after school, after sports, and before eating snacks or meals.

Most kids squirt on a glob of soap and immediately wash it off. Instead, have him wet his hands, turn off the water, lather up, sing "Happy Birthday" twice, turn the water back on, and rinse. This simple trick helps him take the time needed to kill germs.

It might just protect him from another flu season!

39

Gotta Have Faith

Give your youngster the gift of a rich and deep faith.

We all need something to believe in, and your little one will base her future religion almost entirely on what you believe. Yes, you! Studies show whatever faith your daughter has at age 14 will most likely be her belief-system for life.

If you don't really know what you believe, why not? This isn't meant to be any type of criticism aimed at you, but it's just a simple question. Share with your child what you think happens after you die and why. In addition to a much-needed system of right and wrong, people around the world take great comfort and joy in their belief in a higher power. When the flaming arrows of life fall like rain, give your little one a shield to weather the storm.

Please thoughtfully consider some kind of religion or belief-system, define your ideas about it, and share that regularly with your mini-me.

40

End Temper Tantrums

Want to know the best way to end temper tantrums?

It's easy. Simply encourage your child to ramp it up or walk away. You'll need to decide which method works best for you, but both suggestions have proven equally effective on our kids.

Tell her, "Is that all you've got? You can scream louder than that. You can kick harder than that." That is as long as she's not kicking you!

Otherwise, simply walk away when she throws a fit. If you leave your youngster screaming and making a scene, she will eventually realize that no one cares that she is acting like a brat. You need to stick to your guns, though. The second you give into this two foot-terrorist's demands is the same day she decides to do it again in the future. And again, and again, and again.

Just like grown-ups, kids are results oriented. If her shenanigans don't work, she will eventually move on to something else.

At least, we all sure hope she does!

41

Successful Bedtimes

The secret to painless bedtimes is simple if you are consistent and you use these two concepts: routine and a little freedom.

We never, and I mean never, turn off the lights and force our kids to go to sleep. For children preschool age and above, we leave the lights on and let them read, play, and stay up as late as they want. Before you freak out, let me explain.

All of our younger kids go upstairs around 8 p.m. and we let our oldest, who is almost in middle school, stay up until 8:30 p.m. or 9 p.m. Then she goes off to her room, too. Otherwise, the kids use the bathroom, we help them brush their teeth, and my wife and I both give them individual bedtimes. We play a short game, read to them, or give them freebies. Once in a blue moon, our kids can choose to skip individual bedtimes to stay up to watch TV or play a family game.

We keep this routine for two reasons: 1) My wife and I need an hour or so to relax, get work done, or reconnect before our own bedtimes and 2) Our children learn to put themselves to sleep and get some down time as an added bonus. As long as you are strict about not letting them creep out of their rooms once you kiss them goodnight, you should get some much-needed moments to yourselves.

42

Stand Up for Yourself

You should teach your child how to respond appropriately when challenged.

Many parents live by the age-old proverb of "turn the other cheek," and that is important but your daughter needs to learn to stand up for herself as well. Think of it this way—if you teach your youngster to surrender to everyone who opposes her, how will she learn to stand up for herself later in life? Someday, she'll inevitably be offered sex, drugs, and alcohol, and you want her to handle that with flying colors.

Use specific examples, and explain how and when she should defend herself verbally and physically. You don't want to unnecessarily frighten your daughter, but she needs to be aware of some potentially bad situations.

One great way to accomplish this is through martial arts. Kids' karate and Taekwondo promote self-defense and respect. It equips your little kicker to handle some of the insults that come her way. We instruct our daughter to politely ask mean kids to stop, to run away, then to tell a parent or teacher if the behavior continues. If none of that works, she should defend herself.

Your kid needs the tools to stand up to anyone eventually—pushy friends, persuasive dates, bullies, annoying sales people, and possibly even predators.

Please teach your child to lead today and NOT to just follow!

43

Bathroom Talk

Young kids love talking about embarrassing bodily functions and a laundry list of other inappropriate topics we wish they wouldn't.

We use a two-fold approach to this problem. First, he might have legitimate questions and we allow him to ask these in private, as freebies, or when we are in the actual bathroom. He can ask anything about anything, and it's up to you to figure out whether to answer honestly or wait until he is old enough to handle that type of information.

The second part of this comes with punishment for using bad language or talking about inappropriate subjects outside the bathroom. When he chooses to do this, we literally have him clean the toilet.

Our bathrooms were sparkling clean for years until our little guys figured it out!

44

Pick Your Battles

Pick your battles and make sure they are the correct ones.

Some days, your kid is just done and needs a little extra grace. She's sugared out, exhausted, or simply down in the dumps. That's not the right time to dig in your heels and demand perfection. Give her a little break every once in a while. This doesn't mean you should allow lying or defiant behavior, because that's never okay! This simply means allowing her to chew with her mouth open and put her elbows on the table every once in a while.

Just don't make it a habit.

45

Advanced Notice

Please give your child a little advanced notice.

We understand you can't always give five- or even one-minute warnings, but try as often as you can. Imagine you're a four-year-old having the most fun you've had in a month playing outside, and your mom tells you to come in immediately. Waa!!!

Unnecessary battles may arise simply because your child has very different needs and wants (yes, even for television and video games) than you do. How would you feel if someone told you to turn off that nail-biter football game with only ten seconds to go in the fourth?

It's easy to give your child this type of heads-up, and he sure would appreciate a little advanced warning before the electronics, toys, and activities go bye-bye.

My next-door neighbor wisely asks his kids, "Do you want to leave right now or in five minutes?" They usually choose the latter, and he gently reminds them that they agreed to the plan when it's time to go. They're usually just grateful for the extra time.

46

Limit Choices

This is straight out of the book *Love and Logic for Early Childhood*, and it works like a charm. Never be foolish enough to ask your little one, "What do you want for breakfast?"

She'll inevitably say, "Chocolate cake."

Then you have to tell her, "No," and look like an ogre for asking. Give her two or three options at the most and all that suit you.

"Would you like a waffle or eggs for breakfast?" Give her a little time to answer and if she doesn't decide, you get to choose for her. Tell her she will lose her choice if she picks something not on the menu.

If she answers, "I'll take a pancake instead," say, "Okay, since you couldn't choose from the options I gave you, you can have a waffle today."

She'll catch on quickly (like with so many of these ideas), and it'll make your life that much easier.

47

Listen to Your Gut

Teach your son to listen to his gut.

How many times can you look back over your own life when you had a bad feeling and something terrible happened? Demand that your child listens to this weird insight into his own life as well.

It's okay to entertain some false alarms to prove that this instinct is a valuable tool for safety and success. I sure wish I'd listened to my wife's insight on more than a few financial matters. I won't make that mistake again!

Teach your kid to listen to this same helpful nudging.

48

Filters

A water filter keeps all of the big and small junk out of your drinking water. Nobody wants to drink dirty brown water, much the same way nobody wants to be around someone who says whatever is on his mind. Explain to your child today how to always communicate appropriately.

Life is full of situations that require this type of filter. If someone has a birthmark or struggles with his weight, teach your youngster to be sensitive to that. If you don't correct him now, who will?

Kids must *learn* to be sympathetic and kind, and they get this from you. Teach them to reject racism, to not make fun of people with special needs, and to not comment on people who struggle with their appearance. At the very least, help him figure out when it's okay to say the first thing that pops into his head and when it's not.

In fact, instruct your child to work hard every day to protect those who can't protect themselves. The world would be a better place if we all tried!

49

Spelling Bee

Take a few minutes in the car or at the dinner table this week to have a spelling bee.

Choose age-appropriate words and offer a small reward. We generally discourage sugar as a prize, but we also understand the huge temptation it is to use it as motivation. It usually works! Our family regularly holds spelling bees, and the simple desire to be champion has proven to be motivation enough most times.

This is a terrific game for teaching your little speller common and essential words she uses every day. Be aware that some kids are naturally great spellers and some aren't. Don't be discouraged if your oldest needs shorter words than your youngest. This is perfectly normal.

Continue to try to have different siblings to win on different days. Nobody wants to lose five in a row and gets excited about playing number six.

50

Trick or Treat

Use this game to teach your child what's a trick and what's a treat. Get creative and play this regularly as you offer different situations for her to consider.

We cover everything from strangers to email scams with our family. On a serious note, this is a good kid-friendly way to approach the topic of inappropriate behavior. We talk about taking baths at friends' houses and who is allowed to see her private parts—mommy, the doctor, and no one else!

Once again, you don't want to upset your daughter with these make-believe scenarios, but it should open the door to a wide variety of conversations. Help her understand what's acceptable, what's not, and what to look out for.

The treats can be everything from eating cookies offered by a trusted friend's mother to making a profit at a lemonade stand. The treat doesn't always have to be a reward as much as something she understands as positive or helpful.

Learning to tell the difference between a trick and a treat is essential.

51

Life isn't Fair

The cold hard fact is that life isn't fair at all.

Folks who are smarter, work harder, and network better than others tend to be more successful. Confidence, education, and upbringing all factor into how far your offspring will go.

If one sibling gets a snow cone, don't bend over backwards to get a snow cone for all of the other kids. You will quickly see the error of your ways when you buy shoes, eat out, watch a movie and, without a doubt, when you get a smart phone for one child and not another. Tough luck!

The only exception to this rule is spreading wins around to keep all of your kids interested in playing every week. Otherwise, nothing about life is fair. Why waste so much time and energy trying to make your little one think it should be!?!

52

Start a Business

Our friend's daughter started her own business selling cupcakes, and she knows more about economics than most college graduates. She was even featured on *Good Morning America* because of her amazing success. What an excellent learning opportunity!

So we decided to give each of our little bankers $50 on their tenth birthday with the specific goal of starting a business. They can buy things, sell things, or make things. They reap the benefits or suffer the losses of the fruits of their labor.

At any start-up price, why not let your tiny entrepreneur get his first taste of finance by starting a small business? You can advise him and oversee sales to whatever degree you have time, but let him fail or succeed, and learn equally from both.

Our daughter quickly learned that the free help from mom and dad dries up after a while. She realized she needed to pay a portion of the profits to keep the wheels of industry moving forward!

53

Work Ethic

Whatever you do, please give your child a solid work ethic.

If you constantly serve him in an attempt to make sure he is stuffed, satisfied, and spoiled, he'll undoubtedly expect that from you (and from life) in the future. This may come as a shocker, but he won't magically inherit the same work ethic you have when he turns eighteen.

In fact, just the opposite has been happening lately. Parents bend over backwards and work long days to protect their children from serious work, and they elevate entertainment to extraordinary levels. The result? The little ingrates expect everything to come on a silver platter and complain when it doesn't.

Do you really want to raise entitled little bums or hardworking volunteers? Your kid needs to understand that the person who puts in the most hours usually gets the greatest benefits. Give your child the gift of a solid work ethic by putting him to work.

Every one of our kids, from the youngest to the oldest, has age-appropriate chores every day. We know it's easier for you to do all of the work when they are little, but please don't. Unless they learn how to work hard now and have fun doing it, it might never happen.

54

No More Complaining

Want to know how to get your kids to quit griping?

Here is the simple solution. Every time she complains about doing something you ask her to do, assign one additional task. We have a very strict rule that when you complain about work, we immediately toss another job on top of the original. You will be pleasantly surprised how the whining comes to an abrupt and joyful end.

Witness the attitude adjustment unfold before your very eyes as you pile on more chores until she completes the current one with a smile on her face.

Works like a charm!

55

What They Get Away With

The dirty little secret is that all of our kids do whatever they get away with.

If your son yells at your spouse and doesn't get punished, he'll keep doing it. This concept is very important. You can't give in just once or twice, and expect a different result the third time. If your son doesn't listen to your husband when he is asked to do something, he will continue to refuse the next time, and the next, and the next.

If he wakes up and plays with your smart phone until school starts, that's exactly what he thinks will happen every day. If he eats chocolate for breakfast and french fries for dinner, you guessed it.

You're the responsible one in the home, so please take charge of how your little one talks, eats, and acts. Monitor the types of TV shows, movies, and video games as well.

Otherwise, he'll most likely keep doing whatever he gets away with.

56

Get Healthy

Yep, that means you, too. Sorry.

When you exercise, eat healthy, and fix those pesky bad habits of your own, your kids will surely benefit. Contribute to the success of your youngsters by being a better you. It's amazing how much more patient, understanding, and helpful you are after you take care of your own physical and mental needs. This essentially requires making time for yourself.

Just because you're in the parent club doesn't mean you have to spend eighteen years serving, entertaining, and coaching your home team. Please take time today to do the things you want to, so you can be ready when your child needs you most.

If you're stressed out, unhealthy, and unhappy, how do you expect your kid to grow up any different!?!

Lead by example, my friend.

57

Show Them How

Opinions vary deep and wide about discipline, so we'll simply make suggestions and encourage you to handle this difficult aspect of parenting in a consistent and ethical manner.

However, if you have trouble getting your toddler to do small age-appropriate chores, please gently put your hands on his and guide him through the process of the chore. He will soon grow tired of your "help" and do it on his own. If you lightly guide his arms to put away the silverware or pick up his toys, he'll probably catch on pretty fast.

This also works for older kids. The embarrassment of having you hold his hands to accomplish a task should provide enough inspiration for him to do it on his own the next time.

It's a huge help for our whole family to have *everyone* pitching in!

58

Hotseat

Another great game for adolescents involves putting someone on the Hotseat.

Members of our family each take turns asking one person
any suitable question. We start to the right of the person on
the Hotseat and work our way around until everyone gets a
turn.

"What are you the most proud of?"

"What is your favorite food?"

"What do you want to do when you grown up?"

"What bugs you the most?"

The only question we don't allow is, "Who is your favorite person?" for obvious reasons.

Get creative and have fun with it!

59

Value of a Dollar

Another effective way to teach your little spender about money involves giving her choice.

This valuable lesson comes by allowing your child the freedom to decide how much to spend on a given item. Let's say the budget for your daughter's shoes is $30. I understand this may be insultingly high or low but it is just an example, so don't slip a disc. Give your daughter that amount and let her go shopping!

If she has her heart set on name-brand shoes, let her pay the difference. She could even do some chores to earn the extra money necessary. She'll learn she needs to work hard to get what she wants.

If your daughter wants to save a little money by buying less expensive shoes, she gets to keep the change. Then she can see if the discount brand stands up to the competition. She also gets the added benefit of understanding the difference between the cost of generic versus Nike.

The unnecessary battle over which shoes, shirt, or pants to buy is magically solved, but this recommendation does come with a certain age requirement. We'll leave that in your capable hands.

60

Play 60

The NFL has a wonderful campaign called *Play 60*, which encourages children to exercise sixty minutes a day.

Go to *www.nflrush.com/play60* for a great list of suggestions from players with a wide variety of fun ideas. Head outside and toss a football or baseball with your kid. If that's too intense, break out the bikes, a Frisbee, or a kite if the wind is in your favor.

If we're stuck inside, our family holds "Color Races" from the couch to the front door. The kids each pick a color and we call out which gets to go first. "Red, go! Blue, go! Green, go!"

The younger ones usually get a head start but not every time, because we want them to still try hard even if they think they're going to lose. Add another twist by yelling out colors to stop for a moment, too. Remind them that attitude and effort truly are the most important aspects of any competition.

Some healthy modeling from you and your spouse in the area of exercise goes a long way, too.

61

Your Kid's Specialty

Please recognize early on that your child won't be great at *everything*.

She may be terrific at soccer, but she'll probably have some Kryptonite. Even super kids don't do all the things we wish they would perfectly. If that's your goal, you should definitely lighten up sooner than later.

Enjoy your children for exactly who they are—short, fat, skinny, developmentally challenged, or top of the class. Praise her for her strengths and work through her weaknesses. Push too hard and you probably won't like what you get. Don't push hard enough and the results will be equally disappointing.

It's up to you and your spouse to find the balance, but please appreciate every day you get with her!

62

Make Them Cook

So let me get this straight—you are doing your son a huge favor by providing snacks and meals whenever he expects them?

Actually, you aren't helping him at all because he could grow up thinking that delicious food should be readily available whenever he wants. Please let us know how that works out for him and for you!

The result may be unrealistic expectations, poor diet, and a disastrous reliance on fast food. We aren't saying that all meals prepared by others fall short of our lofty standards, but consider this: If your child never experiences food preparation, he just might spend thousands of dollars paying for food that would cost ⅓ or less if he simply made it himself. This idea should be a no-brainer.

Yes, it's messy, and he probably won't get it right when he first starts. It may even take twice as long and result in frustration on your part and his, but if he treats you like a drive-thru window today, that's exactly what he'll expect in his twenties and beyond. It's much harder to eat healthier when you're eating out as well.

Please give both your girls and boys the gift of healthy food preparation skills today.

63

Swap out Toys

One of the best ways to inexpensively keep your daughter entertained is to swap out her toys.

No, we aren't talking about taking away her favorite playthings and making them disappear for a while. That would be cruel and unusual punishment for sure. We humbly suggest taking a few of the toys she doesn't play with very often and splitting them into two or three groups. Every other month, swap them out so your child regularly gets a fresh batch of playthings to enjoy.

This works really well for books, too.

64

Job Interview

You can almost guarantee that your son will sit at an interview one day with high hopes of getting that job. It's never too early to start showing him how to perform to the best of his ability under pressure. We practice at the dinner table and the winner customarily gets out of doing dishes.

Teach your little job seeker how to answer the tough questions like, "What are your strengths?" and "What are your weaknesses?"

Coach him not to ask questions like, "How long are my breaks?" and "Can I use my cell phone on the job?" Those questions come *after* he gets the gig.

Always have him finish by asking, "When can I start?" According to a friend of mine who works in H.R., this is the best way to end any interview. If he doesn't get hired on the spot, tell him to ask, "When may I call if I don't hear back from you by Friday?"

This is another essential step in getting him prepared for the real world.

65

Protect Your Kids

Did you know Cheerios and a dab of milk work better than most super glues? It sure feels like it when I'm cleaning them out of the bowl with a jackhammer, but this is simply another random observation in the middle of important kid destiny work. Let's get back to it.

Please do your best to protect your child from bad friends and mean people. This includes your own family! If your mother is verbally abusive, don't spend much time with her. And if your brother drinks too much and swears around your daughter, politely make other plans for the holidays.

Yes, family is extremely important and you need to have a ton of grace for the shortcomings of all of the special people in your life, but you shouldn't make your kids suffer just because it's a birthday or holiday. Hold yourself, your child, her friends, and *everyone* in her life to a higher standard and protect her from bad characters.

This is a tough topic, but we know you'll ultimately do what's best for her and for you.

66

How to Deal with the Non-Eater

The age-old struggle of how to get your kid to eat remains the same. We'll remedy this issue with one smart move.

She should stay at the table as long as others are eating (or as long as her little attention span can handle), but you shouldn't feel like she needs to finish her entire plate of food at every meal. Plates are huge these days and your little one, for the most part, should be the judge of whether or not she is full.

But here is the kicker: If she isn't hungry and barely touches her dinner, simply put the food in the refrigerator for her to eat the next time she gets hungry. Instead of skipping your healthy meals for those delicious snacks later, she gets leftovers the next time she asks.

Ta-da! Problem solved.

67

He's Standing Right There

All too often, we rush to the rescue when we see our little one frustrated or upset. Why not give him a little extra time, when appropriate, to work through his feelings and figure it out on his own?

If we constantly save him from troubles, our little ray of sunshine won't learn to work through his own problems. You should clearly never leave him in danger or feeling completely helpless, but it's healthy to give your son the chance to figure some things out on his own.

When our boys complain about each other to us, we usually say, "He's standing right there. Why don't you tell him how you feel?" Many times, they work through it on the spot with minimal parental guidance suggested.

There is no hard line as to when to let him work through it and when to help him out, but don't rush to save the day every time. If you do that, he'll never learn to do things for himself.

68

Dealing with Stress

Are you frustrated or carrying work stress into your family relationships? Are finances affecting how you interact with your child? Or are your relationship problems filtering down to your little one?

Your kid is dialed in to more than you think. Protect her from unneeded stress, but share a little of the realities of everyday life with her to prepare her for having her own family. Tell her how you handle issues and give her the tools to do the same.

Hopefully, you can model a healthy marriage, social life, and work ethic to give her an example to follow as she grows up.

69

The Name Game

Our family likes to play a game in the car called, "The Name Game." It's a simple challenge that helps your child learn to deal with pressure situations.

We always pick two names that are off-limits. Otherwise, every other name under the sun can be used. Players go around the circle giving one name at a time. It sounds easy, but it's not.

Anyone playing can count down a three-second timer as each family member tries to think of another name. If the timer gets to zero before he says a name, he is out. The younger children get all the time they need, but no one can say a name twice or say a name that is off limits. If you do, you're out for the rest of that round.

Family, friends, pets, and movie characters are all available, and it's surprising how quickly people flunk out. With literally over a thousand names we can use, the game is usually over within minutes. Keep it light and fun, then talk about how everyone handled the stress afterward.

Discuss how to be a gracious loser as well.

70

Spending, Savings, and Charity

We all know what ridiculous choices kids make when it comes to money, so why not help with a simple plan?

We make it mandatory for our youngsters to take any money they get as gifts, as allowance, or by doing extra chores and split it up three ways: spending, savings, and charity.

Fifty percent goes into spending that she can use any way she chooses. This doesn't mean she can buy a motorcycle or an iPhone without our permission, but we let her purchase nearly everything else no matter how silly. It's her money!

Forty percent goes into savings. It's a terrific way to start teaching your child how to budget properly. If you are consistent for eighteen years, she will have quite the little nest egg for education, a car, or possibly even a small down payment on a home.

Lastly, we ask her to contribute ten percent to charity. Giving to a worthy cause, your local church, or something you pick together helps her get a better understanding of the world around her.

I must admit that this is the most difficult principle for our family to stick to, because our little spenders quickly realized how hard it is to cough up half their dough. Like most things, the more consistent you are, the easier it is for everyone to stick to the plan.

A solid budget for mom and dad is always a good idea, too.

71

The Cardboard Box

One of the greatest toys you can give a small child is a large cardboard box. The bigger the better!

Let her get creative, cut out windows, and use markers. Watch her imagination run wild. Will it be a convertible or an airplane? A horse stable or a castle?

Isn't it funny at Christmas how little ones often enjoy the box more than the actual gift? That's because a box offers endless possibilities, but most toys have only one use.

Why not grab four or five boxes and build a mansion! And leave it up for more than just one day. There should be no rush to tear it down because if the people you invite over for a dinner party don't appreciate it, you may need to find new friends.

It doesn't need to be a permanent addition to your house, but you should have a pretty good idea of when it's the right time to tear it down.

72

Quality Time

You don't have to spend money to enjoy quality time with your children.

All too often, we try to focus family outings around an event—the zoo, a movie, dinner out, and kids' play lands. These are always fun, but it's not required. Parks, the beach, the mountains, and open spaces all provide countless hours of free entertainment if you're willing to hunt for them.

You need to understand that *how often* you play with your children is much more important than *where* you play with them. So get out there and have some fun with your kids this week!

73

Counseling

Sometimes we don't have all the answers. The pressures of life, marriage, money, intimacy, and having kids prove to be too much for us. It's okay to ask for help when you need it.

It's probably less expensive for you to get the counseling you need now instead of dealing with a broken family, divorce, or worse later. If you find yourself turning to unhealthy outlets to manage any of your problems, please consider talking with a professional about it.

Some children have anger, genetic, and psychological issues you simply can't address alone. That's okay! Don't be too proud or too stubborn to ask for some assistance. This book can't even come close to addressing all of the various issues you might face as a parent. Instead of going down with a sinking ship, please consider talking to a counselor.

In the immortal words of Christopher Robin to Winnie the Pooh, "You're braver than you believe, and stronger than you seem, and smarter than you think."

That is true, but sometimes we simply can't find our way out of the valley alone.

74

Chores as Punishment

We talked earlier about having your youngsters help around the home, but my wife and I regularly use chores as punishment, too.

If one child is being disrespectful to another and we witness it, we immediately dish out a small task to curb the behavior. We have him pick up toys or clean the kitchen floor. Always give additional chores if he complains about the first chore as mentioned previously. Hopefully, this won't be the primary reason your house is so darn clean all the time!

Also, have your little one pick up his own toys and dirty clothes. Why are you bending over backwards and cleaning up after him all the time?

Stop it! At a certain young age, he is more than capable.

75

Grocery Planning

You already introduced your little chef to food preparation and clean up, why not include him on the meal planning as well? Open up the cookbook, find your favorite recipes, and talk with your child about everything that goes into cooking, from the store to the kitchen table.

How much does each item cost? What do you have in the pantry and what do you need to buy? We even play a game where our kids guess how much common grocery items cost.

If you have older children, let them plan, buy, and cook an entire meal. Once they conquer that, put them on a budget and try it again. Then have them plan meals for an entire week.

Heck, he might be a better cook than you!

76

Love of Reading

Teach your youngster to love reading!

It is one of the most essential skills for success, and it's easy to encourage. Simply turn off the electronics and set a designated amount of time to read each day. My wife does a great job of taking our kids to the library several times a month as well. We keep those books in one specific area so they don't get mixed up with our personal books. Our little readers get to pick books on any topic they choose, and it really helps motivate them to stay engaged.

Read to your child, encourage her to read on her own, and watch her learn and grow in so many wonderful ways. Her financial future may depend heavily on this one aspect of her upbringing.

77

Munchkins in Your Bed

You're exhausted from life, work, and demanding kids, and when your head finally hits the pillow, you hear it. A crying kid sneaks into your room and curls up for the night. We understand your defenses are down and admit it can be wonderful to snuggle with your little angel but hold that line, soldier!

If your son finds a weakness in your fortress, he will exploit it every time. Make no mistake, having a sick kid or one who just had a nightmare come into your bed for some much-needed comfort is wholly appropriate. Raising a kid who can't sleep in his own bed is not. You're incredibly intelligent and we're confident you'll make the right decision when it comes to this issue.

My wife and I put a "five-minute limit" as well as a "sleep nearby" rule into effect. After making one too many costly mistakes (and waking up with a wet bed more than once), we decided to give him five minutes to hang out before he is banished back to his own room. The other option is pillows and blankets on the floor by our bed if he wants to sleep close to us for just one night.

It works remarkably well, but it's still hard to make anything resembling a good decision when it's four a.m., just like some of you in college!

78

Getting Lost

Lost and Found!

When we vacation with our little travelers, we let them navigate the airport whenever we have the time. We also ask them to find someone with a nametag if they ever get lost. We repeated this instruction several times and we are so thankful we did. When we spent the day at Sea World, we lost our three-year-old son, Ryan.

It was horrible and I remember it like it was yesterday. We were all looking at the Manta Roller Coaster as it passed overhead and when we looked back down, our son was gone. It was four horrifying minutes until they let us know that he was safe and sound with the Sea World staff.

When we got to him, he had a drink, a snack, and a stuffed animal. I later joked that since his free goodies would have cost us about thirty dollars, we should lose our daughter after lunch!

In all seriousness, our boy realized he was lost, remembered what we had told him, walked right up to someone with a nametag, and announced he was M.I.A. You don't want to unsettle your family with too much emergency training, but they sure need the basics.

My little girl later admitted that she saw him wander off, but she didn't follow him because she "didn't want to get lost, too!"

79

Truth or Bologna

This game provides plenty of good laughs even if you don't like the popular lunchmeat.

You get to learn a little more about the wonderful people in your life, and your little detective learns how to tell if someone is lying. One player tells a story and the others have to decide if it's "truth" or "bologna."

The key is to say something the others will guess incorrectly. Find something unbelievable in your past or make up a believable fact, and if the others guess wrong, you get one point. This also provides an excellent opening to talk about body language and deception, and how it can hurt us.

Some of their stories just might surprise you, too.

80

Squelch Interruptions

Don't let your child interrupt anyone! It's rude and unless your little one learns this lesson early, she may never understand it.

If I'm talking to someone or on the phone, and my daughter has something to say, we taught her to place her hand on my arm. Then I'll either stop and listen to her or place my hand on top of hers to show that I've heard her, and she'll get to talk soon enough.

As with most lessons, if you're consistent and firm, your kids will learn to play by the rules most of the time.

81

The Story Generator

Feed your child's imagination by coming up with a story together – one word at a time!

Go back-and-forth or around the table with each person contributing a single word to the adventure. For example, I would start by saying, "A," my son would say "long," my wife would say, "time," and my daughter would say, "ago."

Have fun with it and create some interesting tales in the process.

82

Pets

Most of you already know if you are dog people, cat people, neither, or both. Our humble suggestion would be two-fold about pets.

1) If you don't ever plan to own a dog or a cat, stick to your guns. Why even float the idea unless you fully intend to buy a furry friend? Children don't like being misled or lied to, and the subject of buying a pet almost always ranks at the top of any kid's wish list. Don't toy with his emotions on this topic, please!

2) If you own a pet, actually make your little veterinarian take care of her. Yes, we know you can clean up after Fluffy, feed her, and take care of her better than he can and with a lot less whining, but it teaches him valuable lessons. Don't rob him of learning the expense and energy involved in taking care of a family pet.

Most kids promise to take care of your fur balls in the negotiating process anyway. Let 'em!

83

Computers, Smart Phones, & Tablets

You're an adult and you can do whatever you want when it comes to TV and video games, but too much of any of these things isn't great for kids.

The more time they spend on these types of things, the less attention span they'll have for the slower things in life like school, books, and work. Too much Wi-Fi radiation may not be good for developing young minds either, but we'll let you be the judge of that, too.

Our family does its best to stick to a "book time for screen time" policy. One hour of reading equals an hour of computer or television time. We strive for educational programs as often as possible, but this can be difficult with so many fun options.

Also, we only let our children play with our smart phones in an emergency. They get addicted to them quickly, and we don't want them bugging us all day for them. We don't allow televisions or computers in their rooms right now either, but we'll see how long that lasts. Please pay attention to what they watch, how long they watch, and how it affects them, then make the necessary adjustments.

Your kids will have their own smart phones before you know it, so please teach them good habits now.

84

Too Much Encouragement!?!

It may be hard to believe, but too little or too much encouragement may be bad for your children, too. The book *Called to Teach* by William Yount puts it this way, "Praise should be given in moderation because too little is ineffective and too much is meaningless."[2]

The author recommends giving praise for performance and not simply for participation. "Using frequent, consistent, specific, and immediate reinforcement will direct students toward achieving"[3] the desired skill. If you praise your daughter for every single thing she does, it won't be long before your encouragement means squat to her.

Hold her to high standards, love her anyway when she messes up, and watch her soar!

---

[2] William Yount, *Called to Teach* (Nashville, TN: Broadman & Holeman Publishers, 1998), 78.
[3] Ibid., 78.

85

***

Watch Your Mouth

Called to Teach also has an excellent chapter on recognizing the importance of *how* we say things instead of simply *what* we say. While the author was writing mostly to teachers, it applies to parents as well. Yount suggests using positive language instead of negative language.

Notice the difference in these examples, and start paying attention to how you speak to your nestlings:

Positive Language	Negative Language
Close the door quietly.	*Don't slam the door.*
Quiet down, you're getting too loud.	*Don't make so much noise.*
Sit up straight.	*Don't slouch in your chair.*
Raise your hand if you know the answer.	*Don't shout your answer.*[4]

As often as possible, please try to use positive language. Pretty please!

***

[4] Ibid., 158-159.

86

Monster Gate

Who is responsible for the audio on DVD's!?! Whenever we try to watch a movie after the kids go to bed, the quiet parts are way too quiet and the loud parts are blaring. We end up using subtitles half the time like all of those wonderful hearing impaired folks out there. All films should be tested with a sleeping two-year-old in the next room—Please! Okay, let's continue.

Your children will love playing "Monster Gate!"

Stand with your legs wider than shoulder width, bend down, and slowly clap your hands together in rhythm. Have your little gymnast try to crawl through without getting touched. If you catch him, you get to tickle him.

Your child must judge the timing to get through safely or suffer the delightful consequences!

87

Healthy Snacks

It is so hard to eat healthy, but you should still try.

We do our best to limit sugar at home, but we allow our kids more leeway when they are out. If you simply let your children decide how many sweets they'll eat, most youngsters overdo it every time. We can't say we blame them. Yum!

One thing that helps minimize this is to have a shelf or a drawer in the fridge with some healthy options. You can put cheese slices, berries, cucumber wedges, string cheese, carrots, or grapes they can munch on throughout the day. In the pantry, you could have a basket with nuts, popcorn, pretzels, raisins, trail mix, and low-sugar cereals available. That actually sounds good right now!

Obviously, you should decide the best options for your little snacker, but it's another great way to teach your child healthy eating habits today.

88

Nanny TV Shows

We're not proud of encouraging people to watch *more* television, but we're honest when something works as well as viewing certain types of shows. *Nanny 911* and *Super Nanny*, which no longer air new episodes in the U.S., set our family firmly on the path to great parenting.

Watching old episodes, wherever you can find them, will really help with most common discipline problems. The recurring themes include firm, loving, and consistent discipline from both parents, routines at bedtime, and winning the naughty corner battle.

Our oldest son got in trouble once and wouldn't stay in the penalty box for all the tea in China. Even though we followed the rule of one minute for every year old, he kept sneaking out. We reset the timer to two minutes every time he left for almost an hour. I was so exhausted that I switched with my wife and had her gently walk him back to the naughty corner until I could take over again. When he saw us switch back, he gave in and never left without permission again. Whew!

These shows offer a goldmine of great advice for even the worst behavioral problems. It's the next best thing for most of us who can't afford a real nanny.

89

How to Use the Internet

We live in a brave new world, and one of the most important skills your little explorer can have is the ability to find and sort through information on the Internet.

In addition to teaching your son about the pitfalls of this wonderful technology, he needs to know how to think critically about what he finds. What is the source? What do other websites say about the topic?

Believe it or not, Google could care less about the truth and they charge big bucks for companies to be at the top of their search results. Those companies or individuals don't always have your best interests at heart. Sometimes they manipulate the facts, too. Your kid needs to understand that the Internet is full of misleading posts, bad information, and plain old lies about anything and everything (especially religion and politics).

Raise up little detectives and help them sleuth for the real facts on every topic they search.

90

Shared Journal

Heart-to-heart talks are the best!

Unfortunately, it's usually only when your son is in the mood to share and that may not be very often. What about topics that are too difficult for him to express verbally? Grab a cheap notebook and start a shared journal. Write your youngster a note of encouragement, then end it by letting him know that this is a safe place. He can ask questions or voice concerns, just like freebies.

Write back and forth, use it to work through conflict, discuss important issues, or simply let him know you couldn't be happier that he is in your life.

91

The Importance of a Name

How do you use your son's name? Do you only take his name in vain!?!

If he only hears his full name when he is in trouble (like I often did), he'll associate it with something negative. Unfortunately, that's the only way many kids ever hear it spoken. That stinks for them!

Instill some real pride in your family name instead. Why not tell stories of great ancestors or the high points in your lineage. If you can't go that far back, simply recall the best of your, your parents', and grandparents' history. We regularly hold our kids to a higher standard simply because they share the same last name as we do.

Use the power of a name as a blessing or a curse. The choice is up to you.

92

Funny Voice Memory Game

Few things are more important for your children than remembering your phone number and address. If she gets lost or separated, you want her to know how to respond and get a hold of you. So why not make it fun!

We play a game where we each say my cell phone number in a different kind of voice. We say it in a spooky voice, a silly voice, an angry voice, or a happy voice. Each round of the game has a winner, and whoever has the most points at the end of the game wins. Then move on to your home address and make it into a song instead.

You and your daughter are the real winners as she learns some essential information without the same old boring repetition.

93

Out of the Medicine Cabinet

Little Curious Georges who sneak into the medicine cabinet can get very sick or worse. The best way to fix this is to keep them locked away and to show him pills aren't candy. We accomplish this by allowing our two-year-old to sample a vitamin or two. Yuck!

The vitamins look just like medicine and come in a similar bottle, so we let him taste a calcium tablet or a multivitamin. He hasn't finished one whole vitamin yet, and he spit it in the trash both times he tried them. Just don't use the Flintstone vitamins for this lesson.

Now when we offer him a taste of any vitamin, he quickly refuses. Smart kid!

94

Tickle Island

You've been doing such an amazing job with the tips from this book and with your own ideas that it's time to take a break!

We have a sectional sofa but any small rug or pillow will do. Designate one spot as "Home Base" and another as "Tickle Island." When your child steps foot onto Tickle Island, do your best to catch her and tickle her. If she is on Home Base, she is safe for now.

I like to lie on the carpet and peek over the top of the sofa. In my best ogre voice, I roar, "If you put one foot on *my island*, I'm going to tickle you until your toes fall off!!!"

Yes, it's utterly ridiculous and that's the point!

95

Idle Threats

Ever threatened a punishment you had no intention of doing? I know we sure have and we had to stop.

Parents regularly threaten consequences in an attempt to curtail a certain behavior. "If you do that one more time, we are turning this car around!" The problem comes when you make the mistake of saying something you don't intend to do. You are essentially lying to your trusting toddler. Then when she misbehaves again, she thinks you won't stick to your guns *again*!

So be careful what you promise as punishment and try as often as possible to be a man or woman of your word. If you say you're going to do something if the negative behavior continues, you darn well better do it.

The impact of your future discipline depends on it!

96

Laundry

Oh, yeah! You know where this is going.

We touched on this briefly before, but this is about teaching those little ones some responsibility and making life a little easier for you. Teach your children to do their own stinkin' laundry.

We start at age 9, but the age when your worker bee is ready varies. He will need a little help in the beginning, and he may even shrink some stuff or run out of clean underwear, but guess what – he'll eventually learn the system. You just might find yourself with a little extra time for the other important things in life.

And if your kid has a really busy week, surprise him and do his laundry for him. You'll be the superhero of the day!

97

Mommy & Daddy Dates

Who doesn't love to go on a date!?! Your kids love it, too!

We honestly enjoy getting some one-on-one time with each of our youngsters and it doesn't take much to make them feel like a million bucks. More importantly, it's a time for us to focus on one child without the distraction of other siblings. We want to make sure they have a place to express themselves outside of our four walls. It also shows them that they are a top priority to both of us.

Some of our favorite outings include Happy Meals at McDonald's (yes, we know it's not the healthiest option), a bike ride, a trip to the dollar aisle, or simply running errands with a frozen yogurt stop at the end. Some dates are bigger like tickets to a sporting event or a fancy dinner out. You might just be surprised what they say when it's just the two of you.

Get dressed up and talk about the importance of good manners, too. Our kids regularly ask for Mommy and Daddy Dates, and we hope they never stop!

98

Charge of Your Own Health

Eating too many M&M's makes most people feel sick, so why not teach your kids the consequences of eating poorly? We regularly remind our donut-lovers, "You are in charge of your own health." This means we let them make some mistakes, too.

Talk about your body as if it were a car. Can you put sugar in the gas tank? What happens if you run an automobile without any oil? Before you know it, you'll hear your little one talking about how making poor choices means she'll get an "upset tummy." Your daughter chooses what to eat when you're not around anyway, so why not teach her the reasons *why* she should make good choices.

She'll be more likely to select healthy options when she understands *how* her body works.

99

Blast from the Past

The Question Book by Bob Biehl asks, "What are five of your most rewarding childhood moments that you would like your child to experience?"[5]

What stands out from when you were little? Going to the zoo with your mom or tossing the ball with your dad? Riding bikes to the ocean or camping in the Rocky Mountains?

My greatest moments surprisingly included the little things – playing chess with my dad, talking about life with my super mom, and driving across the country to see our relatives. Who knew driving to Minnesota in December would be one of my favorite childhood recollections!?! Weird, I know.

Now go make some memories based on your old favorites today.

---

[5] Bobb Biehl, *The Question Book* (Nashville, TN: Oliver-Nelson Books, 1993), 210.

100

Expert Advice from Parents.com

Almost done!

Parents.com has a terrific article titled, "The Best Expert Parenting Advice Ever." We'll just share the highlights from the bright folks who work with kids every day.

Preschool Teacher: "If a parent doesn't follow my directions, I'll assume her child won't either… As soon as you break my rules, that creates an immediate bias against your child. And most teachers feel the same way."

Pediatrician: "80 percent of ear infections go away without them (antibiotics). It's a dirty little secret of pediatrics that ear infections pay our bills."

Kids' Dentist: "You may fear dentists, but there's no need to make your kid be afraid of them. Tell him, 'You'll meet some nice people, they'll shine your teeth and count them. They'll have some neat special tools they'll show you.'"

Daycare Director: "At pickup, get off the cell phone, make eye contact, and say hello nicely. It's a long day for a little kid, and he misses you."[6]

This post opened our eyes to quite a few things even though, obviously, not all ear infections go away on their own.

[6] Reshma Yaqub, "The Best Expert Parenting Advice Ever," *Parents.com,* July 2008, http://www.parents.com/parenting/better-parenting/advice/best-expert-parenting-advice/#page=2 (accessed January 19, 2015).

101

Volunteer

Nothing teaches your child to appreciate the world around her like volunteering together.

It can be tough to find these kinds of opportunities with your little one, but it's well worth the effort. Take a meal to an elderly person or help with a neighbor's yard work. Visit a nursing home, wash dishes at a homeless shelter, or simply read books in a needy neighborhood to provide excellent insight into the importance of serving others.

Make the world a better place today by teaching your kid to be grateful for whatever you've got!

Final Thoughts

Raising ankle-biters is crazy and expensive! If most parents knew the heartbreaks, hardships, and heroics required, they may have planned their lives a little differently. Please don't let that stop you, and embrace the chaos.

Yes, kids can be moody, manipulative, and messy, but they're a HUGE blessing, too. Ask any grandparent, and they'll tell you how fast the time goes. It will undoubtedly go better if you put in the work early and often. Remember, your kids get to pick your nursing home so proceed with caution and enjoy the ride.

Please email us suggestions at *GreatKids101@gmail.com*, too. Have fun and good luck. You're gonna need it!

Bibliography

Biehl, Bobb. *The Question Book*. Nashville, TN: Oliver-Nelson Books, 1993.

Fay, Jim & Charles. *Love and Logic Magic for Early Childhood: Practical Parenting from Birth to Six Years*. Golden, CO: Love and Logic Press, 2000.

Mohler, Albert. *The Conviction to Lead*. Bloomington, MN: Bethany House Publishing, 2012.

Yaqub, Reshma. *"The Best Expert Parenting Advice Ever."* *Parents.com,* July 2008.
http://www.parents.com/parenting/better-parenting /advice/best-expertparenting-advice/#page=2 (accessed January 19, 2015).

Yount, William. *Called to Teach*. Nashville, TN: Broadman & Holeman Publishers, 1998.

About the Author

Jim Gromer served as a Search & Rescue Swimmer in the U.S. Navy off the coast of Somalia and in the Persian Gulf before beginning his career in writing and television. His journey includes employment with Starz!, Comcast, and ABC News. Jim is an Emmy-Award winning producer and host of fifteen episodes of the extreme sports show "Rocky Mountain Adventurer."

Jim currently lives in Parker, Colorado with his delightful wife, Rachel, and their four (mostly) well-behaved children. To submit suggestions or to book the author for your next event, please email us at *GreatKids101@gmail.com*.

P.S.—Here is the photo that *didn't* make the book cover.

Which one do you like better?

Index

www.ingramcontent.com/pod-product-compliance
Lightning Source LLC
Chambersburg PA
CBHW020502030426
42337CB00011B/206